Criticism Is a
Legislative Methodology

Criticism Is a
Legislative Methodology

By *Al-Allamah* Rabi' b. Hadi Al-Madkhali

 © Al-Rahmaniyyah Press

ISBN: 979-8-89660127-291-2
First Edition: 1446 AH/December 2024

Published by:

Al-Rahmaniyyah Press
PO Box 8671 Turnersville, NJ 08012 U.S.A.
Electronic mail: editor@alrahmaniyyah.com

Translated by Abu Al-Hasan Malik Al-Akhdar
Reviewed by Abu Suhayl Anwar Wright
Edited by Al-Rahmaniyyah Press
Proofread by Tariq Ben Nuriddin Porter
Cover Art by Al-Rahmaniyyah Press

"By Allah, we are not afraid of criticism because we are not infallible." *–Al-Allamah* Rabi' b. Hadi Al-Madkhali

Table of Contents

Translator's Introduction

S ome seem to despise criticism, especially partisans and people of desires. They blister at the mere mention of a mistake, particularly when their leaders are critiqued. It is as if they believe they are beyond error, that correction and critique are beneath them. This intensifies when *Salafi* scholars or their students are the critics. In response, the partisans accuse them of envy, harshness, or incompetence. The irony is glaring: they take offense at criticism but hurl it freely at the people of *Sunnah*. "They refute others but cannot even recite *Al-Fatihah* properly," they repeat. Perhaps someone should inform them that this, too, is criticism—no different from what they decry.

Over the years, they have claimed that the *Salafis* focus only on *Al-Jarh wa Al-Ta'dil* (the science of Criticism and Praise) while neglecting more important matters. First, this is a blatant lie. Anyone who looks at the lessons, lectures, writings, and translations of the *Salafis* will find an array of subjects: *fiqh*, *tafsir*, *hadith*, Arabic, and more. Yet even the classical works of these sciences include criticism. Did not the grammarians of Basrah and Kufah refute and rebut one another? They even developed a form of critique similar to *Al-Jarh wa Al-Ta'dil* to assess a grammatist's reliability and precision. The same applies to works of *fiqh*. They are replete with observations. Consider *Al-Muhalla* by Ibn Hazm, one of the primary texts of jurisprudence, where he critiques the four schools of *fiqh* throughout.

Second, partisans have no issue with the praise part of *Al-Jarh wa Al-Ta'dil*. They accept it openhandedly, even when undeserved.

Amidst this, I came across the treatise before the reader while living in Arar, Saudi Arabia. Upon reading it, I recognized the importance of translating such a work. I completed a draft and prepared it for publication, but when I returned stateside in 2004, I realized the file had been lost. To Allah we belong, and to Him, we shall return. For years, I put the project aside. But after witnessing so much criticism *of* criticism (more irony), I decided it was high time to re-translate the book and publish it as a defense of this vital methodology.

For our part, we welcome critique, as our *Shaykh* states, "Criticism does not offend us. By Allah, we are happy with it…By Allah, we are not afraid of criticism because we are not infallible."

This is not just lip service from our *Shaykh* but a well-known position and practice, as evident from an official announcement he published thirty-one years ago:

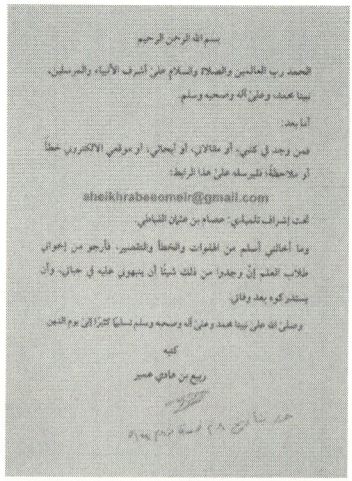

8

All praise is for Allah, Lord of the Worlds, and blessings and peace be upon the noblest of the Prophets and Messengers, our Prophet Muhammad, his family, and his companions.

To proceed:

Whoever finds an error or issue in my books, articles, research, or website, please send it to this address:

sheikhrabeeomeir@gmail.com

Under the supervision of my student, 'Isam b. 'Uthman al-Qabati.

And I do not think I am immune from mistakes and shortcomings. So, I ask my brothers, the students of knowledge, if they find anything of that, to inform me of it in my life and correct it after my death.

May Allah abundantly bless our Prophet Muhammad (ﷺ), his family, and companions until the Day of Judgment.

Written by

Rabi' b. Hadi 'Umayr

Dated on the 28th of Jumada Al-Ula, 1415 AH

His humility and commitment to truth are evident. Here is an *imam* of the *Sunnah* openly inviting students of knowledge to highlight mistakes or oversights in his works.

In contrast, many people become angry over corrections as minor as typographical errors, let alone issues in creed, methodology, or interpretation. They should welcome critique so that they might repent and correct the error of their ways before meeting their Lord.

May Allah guide us and them to understand that perfection belongs to Him alone and that criticism is essential. It has played a singular role in preserving our faith. The *Sunnah* of His Messenger (ﷺ) and the creed of the *Salaf* would not have reached us without it.

Written by one in need of his Lord's pardon,

Abu Al-Hasan Malik Al-Akhdar
6 Jumada Al-Thani 1446 AH
Camden, NJ

Criticism is a Legislative Methodology

All praise is due to Allah, and may peace and blessings be upon the Messenger of Allah (ﷺ). To proceed:

Enjoining what is right and forbidding what is wrong is one of the distinguishing features of this *Ummah* and among the greatest duties. One cannot establish the religion without it.

Clarifying the truth to people and not concealing it is a significant matter, with a great promise of reward for those who convey knowledge and teach the religion of Allah. Conversely, there is a severe warning for those who conceal it. He says,

﴾إِنَّ ٱلَّذِينَ يَكْتُمُونَ مَآ أَنزَلْنَا مِنَ ٱلْبَيِّنَٰتِ وَٱلْهُدَىٰ مِنۢ بَعْدِ مَا بَيَّنَّٰهُ لِلنَّاسِ فِى ٱلْكِتَٰبِ أُوْلَٰٓئِكَ يَلْعَنُهُمُ ٱللَّهُ وَيَلْعَنُهُمُ ٱللَّٰعِنُونَ﴾

"Indeed, those who conceal what We sent down of clear proofs and guidance after We made it clear for the people in the Scripture—those are cursed by Allah and cursed by those who curse" (*Al-Baqarah* 2:159).

This issue is often contested by people of innovation, misguidance, and *Sufism*, who view it as backbiting. There is no question that backbiting is impermissible and that the Muslim's honor, blood, and wealth are inviolable. The Messenger of Allah (صَلَّى اللهُ عَلَيْهِ وَعَلَى آلِهِ وَسَلَّمَ) addressed this matter in his sermon on the Day of Sacrifice (*Eid al-Adha*), as narrated by Abu Bakrah.[1] He said,

«أَتَدْرُونَ أَيُّ يَوْمٍ هَذَا؟»، قُلْنَا: اللهُ وَرَسُولُهُ أَعْلَمُ، فَسَكَتَ حَتَّى ظَنَنَّا أَنَّهُ سَيُسَمِّيهِ بِغَيْرِ اسْمِهِ، قَالَ: أَلَيْسَ يَوْمَ النَّحْرِ؟ قُلْنَا: بَلَى، قَالَ: أَيُّ شَهْرٍ هَذَا؟، قُلْنَا: اللهُ وَرَسُولُهُ أَعْلَمُ، فَسَكَتَ حَتَّى ظَنَنَّا أَنَّهُ سَيُسَمِّيهِ بِغَيْرِ اسْمِهِ، فَقَالَ أَلَيْسَ ذُو الْحِجَّةِ؟، قُلْنَا: بَلَى، قَالَ أَيُّ بَلَدٍ هَذَا؟ قُلْنَا: اللهُ وَرَسُولُهُ أَعْلَمُ، فَسَكَتَ حَتَّى ظَنَنَّا أَنَّهُ سَيُسَمِّيهِ بِغَيْرِ اسْمِهِ، قَالَ أَلَيْسَتْ بِالْبَلْدَةِ الْحَرَامِ؟ قُلْنَا: بَلَى، قَالَ: فَإِنَّ دِمَاءَكُمْ وَأَمْوَالَكُمْ عَلَيْكُمْ حَرَامٌ، كَحُرْمَةِ يَوْمِكُمْ هَذَا، فِي شَهْرِكُمْ هَذَا، فِي بَلَدِكُمْ هَذَا.»

"Which day is this?" They said, "Allah and His Messenger know best." He was silent until we thought he might give it a different name. Then he said, "Is it not the Day of Sacrifice?" We said, "Yes, Messenger of Allah." He then asked, "Which month is this?" We replied, "Allah and His Messenger know best." He was silent until we thought he might give it a different name. Then he said, "Is it not the the sacred month?"

---

[1] **TN:** In the original Arabic version, it reads "Abu Bakr," but it appears that the narrator is Abu Bakrah, Nufay' b. Harith. May Allah be pleased with him. And Allah knows best.

We said, "Yes, Messenger of Allah." Finally, he asked, "Which town is this?" We said, "Allah and His Messenger know best." He remained silent until we thought he might give it a different name. Then he said, "Is it not the Sacred Precincts?" We said, "Yes, Messenger of Allah." The Prophet (ﷺ) then declared, "Indeed, your blood, your property, and your honor are as sacred to each other as this day, in this month, in this city."[1]

Allah says,

﴿يَٰٓأَيُّهَا ٱلَّذِينَ ءَامَنُواْ ٱجۡتَنِبُواْ كَثِيرٗا مِّنَ ٱلظَّنِّ إِنَّ بَعۡضَ ٱلظَّنِّ إِثۡمٞۖ وَلَا تَجَسَّسُواْ وَلَا يَغۡتَب بَّعۡضُكُم بَعۡضًاۚ أَيُحِبُّ أَحَدُكُمۡ أَن يَأۡكُلَ لَحۡمَ أَخِيهِ مَيۡتٗا فَكَرِهۡتُمُوهُۚ﴾

"O you who have believed, avoid much [negative] assumption. Indeed, some assumption is sin. And do not spy or backbite each other. Would one of you like to eat the flesh of his brother when dead? You would detest it" (*Al-Hujarat* 49:12).

Without question, the Muslims' honor is sacrosanct, and eating their flesh is like eating the flesh of a dead person. Who could tolerate this? Indeed, a [pure] soul would reject it. However, for the sake of Islamic interests and the preservation and

---

[1] Collected by Al-Bukhari in his *Sahih* (no. 4406), Muslim in his *Sahih* (no. 1679), Ibn Majah in his *Sunan* (no. 233), *Imam* Ahmad in his *Musnad* (no. 19936), and Al-Darimi (no. 1916).

protection of this religion, Allah has permitted certain matters that, although they may outwardly resemble backbiting, they are not. A person makes mistakes, and we must point them out. This is called advice or clarification, a fundamental principle in Islam that must be upheld so that the religion is not lost. Given how often people err, fall into mistakes, or are misled by desires. May Allah protect us. Even some of the righteous can be led by their desires, sometimes being overcome by them, causing them to make mistakes and speak about Allah without knowledge.

Among the distinctions of this *Ummah*, which make it superior to other nations, is that it is commanded to enjoin what is right and forbid what is wrong. Allah has promised to preserve this religion, as He says,

$$ \text{﴿ إِنَّا نَحْنُ نَزَّلْنَا ٱلذِّكْرَ وَإِنَّا لَهُۥ لَحَٰفِظُونَ ﴾} $$

"Indeed, it is We who sent down the Reminder, and indeed, We will be its guardian." (*Al-Hijr* 15:9)

So Allah preserved [the religion] through this nation, which He praised, saying about it,

$$ \text{﴿ كُنتُمْ خَيْرَ أُمَّةٍ أُخْرِجَتْ لِلنَّاسِ تَأْمُرُونَ بِٱلْمَعْرُوفِ وَتَنْهَوْنَ عَنِ ٱلْمُنكَرِ وَتُؤْمِنُونَ بِٱللَّهِ ﴾} $$

"You are the best nation raised up for mankind. You enjoin what is right and forbid what is wrong and believe in Allah" (*Ali Imran* 3:110).

Thus, enjoining what is right and forbidding what is wrong includes correcting, clarifying, and explaining mistakes to the people. This is part of enjoining good and forbidding evil and helps to keep people steadfast in the religion of Allah, preserving it from the distortions of the ignorant and the false claims of the misguided. While people's honor is protected, is it protected in all cases? If someone goes astray, makes mistakes, commits adultery, or commits murder, is his life, wealth, and honor still entirely protected? Those who argue this might say that a murderer should not be executed, a thief's hand should not be cut, an innovator should not be refuted, and a person in error should not be corrected—all because Allah has prohibited violation of your lives and wealth. But this is a misunderstanding and deviation in the religion of Allah that exposes it to ruin.

The *Sufis* used to object to the scholars of *hadith*, saying, 'Why do you say that so-and-so has a poor memory or that so-and-so is a liar? Are you not backbiting people?' The *muhaddithun* responded, 'This is not backbiting. This is advice. This is clarification for the people and has nothing to do with backbiting.

15

Thus, we find that the Messenger of Allah (ﷺ) was the most pious of people and the most fearful of Allah. At the same time, he was the foremost advisor, not fearing anyone but Allah. The Prophet (ﷺ) did not backbite or malign anyone. However, when the time came, he clarified and advised.

It is essential to understand this religion and to distinguish between forbidden backbiting and slander—Allah protect us—and between sincere advice and clarification, which Allah has entrusted to this *Ummah*. This form of criticism serves as a safeguard to protect this religion and fulfills Allah's promise to preserve it. He says,

﴿ إِنَّا نَحْنُ نَزَّلْنَا ٱلذِّكْرَ وَإِنَّا لَهُۥ لَحَٰفِظُونَ ﴾

"Indeed, it is We who sent down the Reminder, and indeed, We will be its guardian." (*Al-Hijr* 15:9)

Allah guided jurists to establish principles for the religion. These principles directly link the interpretation of rulings to religious texts. They established the principles of jurisprudence that help us distinguish between the abrogating and the abrogated texts, the unrestricted and the restricted, and other foundational principles. These principles guide us in deriving rulings and deepening our understanding of Allah's religion.

Understanding abrogation is a vast field supported by abundant evidence, with some texts indicating abrogation, others restricting previously unrestricted texts, and still others specifying general ones. *Imam* Al-Shafi'i established this science, followed by other esteemed scholars of Islam. May Allah grant them mercy. No one questioned the importance of this knowledge, and all praise is for Allah, as it is essential. It is grounded in the Arabic language, the Qur'an, and the *Sunnah*, making the principles of jurisprudence firmly based on these sources.

Allah preserved this religion through principles established by Islamic scholars to distinguish authentic narrations from weak ones and identify reliable narrators from unreliable ones. These principles were implemented using statements such as, 'So-and-so is trustworthy,' 'So-and-so is a liar,' 'So-and-so has poor memory,' and so forth. [The scholars] classified narrators, documented them, and applied these criteria to assess their reliability. Thus, we accept the narrations of reliable, trustworthy transmitters, in line with the conditions they set for determining authenticity: a report from trustworthy and precise narrators, with an unbroken chain, free from hidden defects and contradictions. This principle effectively excludes the liars, misguided innovators—although some innovators' narrations are accepted in cases of necessity—and also excludes those with severe errors, poor memory, broken chains, and similar issues. Scholars of this field have clarified these matters to distinguish between sound and weak narrations and between [trustworthy and untrustworthy] narrators.

These principles enabled scholars to evaluate narrators and produce works encompassing tens of thousands of transmitters. [They would say], "This one is trustworthy and precise," "This one is a liar and a forger," "This one has a poor memory," "This one is accused of lying," "This one often relates broken chains (*marasil*),"[1] "This one is *mudallis*,"[2] and so on. So, if I said a person is *mudallis*, is this considered backbiting? When *Imam* [Sufyan] Al-Thawri said, "So and so is *mudallis*," is this backbiting? The misguided, ignorant *Sufis* consider this backbiting, but to the scholars of Islam, it is sincere advice and necessary clarification for the people. Through such advice and clarification, we preserve Allah's religion.

---

[1] **TN:** A *mursal hadith* occurs when a *Tabi'i* omits the name of an intermediary between him and the Prophet. An example is when Sa'id b. Al-Musayyib or another *Tabi'i* says, "The Messenger of Allah said or did," without mentioning who narrated it to them. The *mursal hadith* is classified as a weak *hadith*.

[2] **TN:** *Tadlis* occurs when a narrator reports a *hadith* in a way that makes it seem as though he heard it directly from his *Shaykh* when, in fact, he did not. Instead, he heard it through an intermediary. Rather than saying, "My *Shaykh* told me," he uses a vague phrase like "So-and-so said," giving the impression of direct transmission.

Malik, Ahmad, Sufyan al-Thawri, Al-A'mash, Al-Awza'i, and before them Yahya b. Ma'in, Yahya b. Sa'id al-Qattan, 'Abd al-Rahman b. Mahdi, 'Ali b. al-Madini, al-Bukhari, and Muslim—all of these scholars, may Allah have mercy on them, critiqued and praised transmitters, spoke out, and authored works on weak and abandoned reporters. They would say, "So-and-so is abandoned," "So-and-so is a forger," "So-and-so is truthful," "So-and-so is trustworthy," "So-and-so is a leading authority," and so on, all to clarify the truth. They even critiqued the children of the Companions, members of *Quraysh*, descendants of the *Muhajirun*, the *Ansar*, and the noble families of 'Umar, Abu Bakr, Ali, and the household of the Prophet (صَلَّ اللَّهُ عَلَيْهِ وَعَلَى آلِهِ وَسَلَّمَ). They did not shy away from critiquing contemporaries of Abu Hanifah, those before him, and those after him. Some even assessed their own fathers, as [Ali] b. al-Madini said, "This is Allah's religion. My father is weak." Similarly, the grandsons of Abu Shaybah, Muhammad b. 'Abd Allah and his brother 'Uthman, would say of their grandfather Abu Shaybah, "He is weak." They did not avoid speaking out because of kinship. They were eminent scholars and prolific writers. Consider Abu Bakr b. Abi Shaybah, the author of *Al-Musannaf* and *Al-Musnad*, as well as several other notable works. *Al-Musannaf* alone would suffice as his legacy. Did he object when his grandfather was labeled weak or attempt to defend him? No. Even if he were offended, would people have listened to him? He would have lost all credibility.

19

If he had objected, saying, "Why do you speak about my grandfather?"—his grandfather was a judge, a prominent figure, but he was weak in *hadith*, so they disregarded him. Even his own sons testified he was weak.

'Ali b. Al-Madini was once asked about his father. He said, "Ask someone else." But they insisted, "We are asking you." He was silent for a moment, then said, "My father is weak." Is this backbiting? Was he being disrespectful by speaking about his father? According to the *Sufis* and those ignorant today who reject criticism, this would be seen as disrespect. How could he talk about his own father? But is his father greater than Islam, Allah's *Dīn*? This is Allah's religion.

Thus, this kind of criticism and clarification appears in the Qur'an.

They say, "Now there are disbelievers, communists, secularists, and threats surrounding the *Ummah*, and we are speaking against one another. Let us stop this talk." So, you call to misguidance, promote innovations, and distort the religion of Allah. How can we remain silent about that? You mention the disbelievers, yet you have done nothing to counter them whatsoever.

The Companions who fought against Quraysh in the decisive Battle of Badr, the battle that changed the course of Islamic history—what was revealed about the Companions of Allah's Messenger?

They were few—just over three hundred—surrounded by a vast sea of *kufr*, with disbelievers from among the Arabs, Persians, Romans, and the people of Hind encircling them. Despite their small numbers, Allah sent down a barrage of criticism upon them. They disagreed about the spoils of war, so Allah revealed,

﴿يَسْتَلُونَكَ عَنِ ٱلْأَنفَالِ قُلِ ٱلْأَنفَالُ لِلَّهِ وَٱلرَّسُولِ فَٱتَّقُوا ٱللَّهَ وَأَصْلِحُوا ذَاتَ بَيْنِكُمْ وَأَطِيعُوا ٱللَّهَ وَرَسُولَهُ إِن كُنتُم مُّؤْمِنِينَ﴾

"They ask you about the spoils of war. Say, 'The spoils are for Allah and the Messenger. So, fear Allah and repair what is between you and obey Allah and His Messenger, if you are indeed believers.'" (*Al-Anfal* 8:1)

One says, "I fought," and another says, "I did this," and another claims, "I am more deserving." Allah then revealed, "The spoils of war are for Allah and His Messenger." Before that, as they set out, the Messenger of Allah (ﷺ) told them that a caravan from Quraysh was on its way, and they should go out, hoping Allah might grant them its spoils. They set out with this intention, not for battle. Then, the Messenger (ﷺ) learned Quraysh was approaching to protect the caravan. What should he do? The Prophet (ﷺ) did

21

not have knowledge of the unseen to know that Quraysh would come out to defend and fight for the caravan. Quraysh came out in full force, not only to rescue the caravan but ready for battle. Abu Sufyan sent word to Abu Jahl and the leaders of Quraysh, "The caravan is safe, so turn back." The wise men of Quraysh—'Utbah b. Rabi'ah, Shaybah b. Rabi'ah, al-Akhnas b. Shurayq, and others—said, "Let us return." But Abu Jahl said, "We will not turn back until we kill them at Badr, make the women sing for us, and drink wine, so our names will ring out among the Arabs." He continued inciting them until they resolved to fight. So, what could the Messenger do? He consulted [his companions], yet some of them argued with him about engaging in battle. [Allah then revealed]:

﴿ يُجَٰدِلُونَكَ فِى ٱلْحَقِّ بَعْدَ مَا تَبَيَّنَ كَأَنَّمَا يُسَاقُونَ إِلَى ٱلْمَوْتِ وَهُمْ يَنظُرُونَ ﴾

"Disputing with you concerning the truth after it was made manifest, as if they were being driven to death, while they were looking (at it)" (*Al-Anfal* 8:6).

Look at this criticism directed toward the Companions. Some said, "We have no equipment for battle. We were not prepared for it," while the Messenger (صَلَّى ٱللَّهُ عَلَيْهِ وَعَلَىٰ آلِهِ وَسَلَّمَ) was determined to engage. He consulted Abu Bakr and 'Umar, who both said, "We will fight." Al-Miqdad then said, "By Allah, O Messenger of Allah, if you commanded us to go to Bark al-Ghimad, we would fight. By Allah, if you plunged into this sea, we would plunge in with you." The morale of some Companions lifted after this, following their debates and exchanges.

This was a critique of the Companions of Allah's Messenger (ﷺ). The Qur'an could have remained silent [about this]. One might ask, what difference would it make if it had? But this was a powerful lesson with a lasting impact on the lives of the Companions. May Allah be pleased with them. Often, the Messenger of Allah (ﷺ) would hint about expeditions, taking [the Companions] out without clarifying whether there would be fighting. Then, he would reveal the enemy's presence, and they would engage without argument, debate, or hesitation.

After Allah aided His Messenger (ﷺ) and gave him victory over his adversaries, killing seventy from the Quraysh and taking seventy as captives, they set out towards Madinah with them. The Messenger of Allah (ﷺ) said, "What do you think of these captives?" He also said, "By Allah, if Mut'im b. 'Adi were alive and asked me for these foul people, I would give them to him."[1] He then asked, "What is your opinion, Abu Bakr? And yours, 'Umar?"

Abu Bakr and some of the people said, "O Messenger of Allah, they are our people and our kin. We should take ransom from

---

[1] Collected by Al-Bukhari in his *Sahih* (nos. 3139 and 4024) and Ahmad in his *Musnad* (no. 27546).

23

them to strengthen ourselves and seek help from it, and perhaps Allah will guide them to Islam one day." 'Umar said, "O Messenger of Allah, these are the leaders of the Quraysh. I do not share Abu Bakr's view. I think you should allow us to rid ourselves of them and eradicate their evil, for these are the leaders of the Quraysh. If we kill them, disbelief will not prevail." The Messenger of Allah (ﷺ) favored Abu Bakr's opinion and accepted the ransom. The next day, 'Umar found the Prophet (ﷺ) and Abu Bakr weeping. 'Umar said, "Why are you both weeping? If I see a reason to weep, I will do so. Otherwise, I will make myself weep." The Messenger of Allah (ﷺ) said, "I weep for what was offered to your people. By Allah, I saw their torment near this tree." This *hadith* is in *Sahih Muslim*.[1]

Then Allah revealed,

$$\text{﴿مَا كَانَ لِنَبِيٍّ أَن يَكُونَ لَهُ أَسْرَىٰ حَتَّىٰ يُثْخِنَ فِى ٱلْأَرْضِ تُرِيدُونَ عَرَضَ ٱلدُّنْيَا وَٱللَّهُ يُرِيدُ ٱلْآخِرَةَ وَٱللَّهُ عَزِيزٌ حَكِيمٌ﴾}$$

"It is not for a prophet to take captives until he has thoroughly subdued the land. You desire the spoils of this

---

[1] Collected by Muslim in his *Sahih* (no. 1764), Al-Tirmidhi in his *Jami'* (no. 3081), Abu Dawud in his *Sunan* (no. 2690), and Ahmad in his *Musnad* (nos. 208 and 221).

world, but Allah desires [for you] the Hereafter. And Allah is Exalted in Might and Wise." (*Al-Anfal* 8:67)

﴿ لَّوْلَا كِتَـٰبٌ مِّنَ ٱللَّهِ سَبَقَ لَمَسَّكُمْ فِيمَآ أَخَذْتُمْ عَذَابٌ عَظِيمٌ ﴾

"If not for a decree from Allah that preceded, you would have been touched for what you took by a great punishment" (*Al-Anfal* 8:68).

This is a guidance for the Messenger of Allah (صَلَّى ٱللَّهُ عَلَيْهِ وَعَلَىٰ آلِهِ وَسَلَّمَ) and his companions. The Prophet (صَلَّى ٱللَّهُ عَلَيْهِ وَعَلَىٰ آلِهِ وَسَلَّمَ) and Abu Bakr chose to accept the ransom, while 'Umar held a different opinion, and who turned out to be correct? 'Umar.

Many verses offer this type of criticism: Christians, Jews, and polytheists are criticized, as well as the companions and the hypocrites. Several verses provide clarification, critique, and explanation, and there is much of this in the *Sunnah*.

For example, Allah says,

﴿ عَفَا ٱللَّهُ عَنكَ لِمَ أَذِنتَ لَهُمْ حَتَّىٰ يَتَبَيَّنَ لَكَ ٱلَّذِينَ صَدَقُواْ وَتَعْلَمَ ٱلْكَـٰذِبِينَ ﴾

"May Allah forgive you. Why did you grant them leave until it became clear to you who were truthful and you knew the liars?" (*Al-Tawbah*: 9:43).

This was an *ijtihad* from the Prophet (ﷺ). The hypocrites came making excuses, saying, "O Messenger of Allah, I have such-and-such," and others said, "I am ill," and the Prophet (ﷺ) excused them. All these excuses were lies, so Allah revealed this verse, "May Allah forgive you," meaning this is a timeless lesson for the Messenger of Allah (ﷺ) and for the *Ummah*. Then Allah revealed [other verses] concerning the hypocrites.

﴿ٱسْتَغْفِرْ لَهُمْ أَوْ لَا تَسْتَغْفِرْ لَهُمْ إِن تَسْتَغْفِرْ لَهُمْ سَبْعِينَ مَرَّةً فَلَن يَغْفِرَ ٱللَّهُ لَهُمْ﴾

"Whether you ask forgiveness for them (hypocrites) or ask not forgiveness for them (and even) if you ask seventy times for their forgiveness, Allah will not forgive them" (*Al-Tawbah* 9:80).

When 'Abd Allah b. Ubayy died, his son 'Abd Allah came and said, "O Messenger of Allah, my father has passed away, and I would like you to shroud him with your garment." The Prophet (ﷺ) agreed. They took him out, and the Messenger (ﷺ) took his garment, shrouded him with it, sat him up on his knees, shrouded him, perfumed him, placed him in the grave, and buried him. When he stood to pray over him, 'Umar said, "O Messenger of Allah, will you pray for him"—and he held the Prophet's garment—"even though he said such-and-such on such a day, and did such-and-such on another day?" The Prophet (ﷺ) replied, "Indeed, Allah has given me a choice," and stated,

﴿ٱسْتَغْفِرْ لَهُمْ أَوْ لَا تَسْتَغْفِرْ لَهُمْ إِن تَسْتَغْفِرْ لَهُمْ سَبْعِينَ مَرَّةً فَلَن يَغْفِرَ ٱللَّهُ لَهُمْ﴾

'Whether you ask forgiveness for them (hypocrites) or ask not forgiveness for them (and even) if you ask seventy times for their forgiveness, Allah will not forgive them' (*Al-Tawbah* 9:80).

"By Allah, if I knew that seeking forgiveness for him over seventy times would cause Allah to forgive him, I would do so."[1]

The Prophet (ﷺ) understood this to be a choice. Then Allah revealed,

﴿وَلَا تُصَلِّ عَلَىٰ أَحَدٍ مِّنْهُم مَّاتَ أَبَدًا وَلَا تَقُمْ عَلَىٰ قَبْرِهِ﴾

"And never pray for any of them who die, nor stand at his grave" (*Al-Tawbah* 9:84).

And He said,

﴿مَا كَانَ لِلنَّبِيِّ وَٱلَّذِينَ ءَامَنُوٓاْ أَن يَسْتَغْفِرُواْ لِلْمُشْرِكِينَ وَلَوْ كَانُوٓاْ أُوْلِى قُرْبَىٰ﴾

"It is not (proper) for the Prophet and those who believe to ask Allah's Forgiveness for the *Mushrikun* (polytheists, idolaters, pagans, disbelievers in the Oneness of Allah) even though they be of kin" (*Al-Tawbah* 9:113).

---

[1] Collected by Al-Bukhari (no. 4469), Muslim (nos. 2494 and 2779), Al-Tirmidhi (no. 3092), An-Nasa'i (nos. 1983 and 1995), Ibn Majah (no. 1454), and Ahmad *Al-Musnad* (no. 4893).

27

All of this serves as guidance, even for the Messenger (ﷺ). This means that the actions of the Prophet (ﷺ) are not approved if they do not align with Allah's will. When an *ijtihad* (independent judgment) contained an error, Allah would provide guidance and correction. It cannot be said that this caused harm to the person of Muhammad (ﷺ), nor did he say, "I am the Messenger of Allah, and no one should object to me." If the Messenger of Allah were to conceal anything, he would have concealed these things, as Aishah said, "If Muhammad were to conceal anything, he would have concealed this verse,

﴿وَإِذْ تَقُولُ لِلَّذِى أَنْعَمَ ٱللَّهُ عَلَيْهِ وَأَنْعَمْتَ عَلَيْهِ أَمْسِكْ عَلَيْكَ زَوْجَكَ وَٱتَّقِ ٱللَّهَ وَتُخْفِى فِى نَفْسِكَ مَا ٱللَّهُ مُبْدِيهِ وَتَخْشَى ٱلنَّاسَ وَٱللَّهُ أَحَقُّ أَن تَخْشَىٰهُ﴾

'And [remember] when you said to the one on whom Allah bestowed favor and you bestowed favor, 'Keep your wife and fear Allah,' while you concealed within yourself that which Allah was to disclose. And you feared the people, while Allah has more right that you fear Him'" (*Al-Ahzab* 33:37).

In the case of Zaynab[1], look at this critique directed at the noble Prophet (ﷺ).

---

[1] Collected by Al-Bukhari (no. 4782), Muslim (no. 177), Al-Tirmidhi (no. 3213), and Ahmad *Al-Musnad* (nos. 22623, 22940, 22631, and 23916).

28

The companions would criticize one another and respond to one another's opinions. Even women would critique. Aishah used to critique and correct others. Al-Zarkashi even compiled a book about her corrections and critiques of the Companions. 'Umar was criticized. He was critiqued by 'Imran b. Husayn, 'Ali b. Abi Talib, and others. 'Umar himself would critique, and as *Imam* Malik said, everyone's words can be accepted or rejected.

Then came Malik, criticizing his teachers, scholars, and others, pointing out their flaws, correcting their mistakes, and evaluating their reliability. The great *imams* followed this tradition, producing numerous and extensive works on the subject.

Criticism serves to purify the people. It may involve critiquing a person, pointing out their errors, or exposing their misguidance. Islam has established these principles, forbidding the violation of wealth, life, and honor, as we mentioned. However, the shedding of blood is permitted in specific cases: for someone who has committed murder, an adulterer, or someone who abandons their religion and separates from the congregation (*jama'ah*). In these circumstances, their blood may be lawfully spilled.[1]

---

[1] **TN:** These matters return to the rulers and proper authorities for implementation, not the common people, as these are concerns of great

Therefore, when someone makes a mistake or goes astray, their reputation may be called into question. However, this must be done with the intention of offering sincere advice for the sake of Allah, and the one giving the advice should aim to clarify the truth and warn the people against falling into error or misguidance. These conditions are essential.

We say that the Qur'an contains extensive correction of the Messenger (ﷺ), the Companions, and others, including polytheists, disbelievers, hypocrites, and more. This criticism in the Qur'an stems from enjoining good, forbidding evil, and clarifying errors to reveal the truth.

We say that the scholars of Islam understood this [responsibility] and established principles in the sciences of the *usul* and *hadith* to preserve the Qur'an, which Allah has promised to protect:

$$﴿ إِنَّا نَحْنُ نَزَّلْنَا ٱلذِّكْرَ وَإِنَّا لَهُۥ لَحَٰفِظُونَ ﴾$$

"Indeed, it is We who sent down the Reminder, and indeed, We will be its guardian." (*Al-Hijr* 15:9)

---

caution. Clarifying this, *Al-Allamah* 'Abd Al-Aziz b. Baz said, "A Muslim must be cautious of the causes of aggression and bloodshed to prevent a disaster with serious consequences," 'Abd Al-Aziz b. Baz, "*Min Hadith La Yuhill Dam Muslim*," accessed December 9, 2024, www.binbaz.org.

Allah prepared this *Ummah* to safeguard the religion. One scholar writes about language to serve the Qur'an, another writes on eloquence and rhetoric, another focuses on the principles of jurisprudence, another on Islamic law, another on the study of narrators, and yet another on abrogation and abrogated verses. All these efforts are means through which Allah has preserved this religion.

This discussion relates to the concept of criticism. Consider how many works *hadith* scholars have written critiquing narrators. How many times have jurists debated and refuted each other's opinions? How often have scholars of Islamic principles and linguists responded to one another? All of this was done to serve Islam and clarify the truth. Through these sincere efforts—Allah willing—this aim has been achieved. While there may have been individuals who lacked sincerity, most of the scholars of this *Ummah*, Allah willing, were characterized by sincerity, honesty, and earnest advice. All these efforts are part of Allah's plan to fulfill His promise to preserve this religion. This is what sets this *Ummah* apart from others, as it is the best nation raised for mankind, enjoining good and forbidding evil.

We say that this methodology of critique is a fair principle applied to everyone, even those from the family of the Messenger of Allah (ﷺ), the family of Abu Bakr, the family of 'Umar, or the families of the *Muhajirun* and *Ansar*. No one was shown favoritism. A person might critique his brother, his father, or his son. All of this was done as sincere advice for the sake of Allah, to clarify the truth, and to warn against mistakes and deviations. All these efforts contribute to preserving Allah's religion.

The distinguishing feature of this *Ummah*, from its beginning until the Day of Judgment, is that there will always remain a group of Muslims who are steadfast upon the truth:

«لَا تَزَالُ طَائِفَةٌ مِنْ أُمَّتِي عَلَى الْحَقِّ ظَاهِرِينَ لَا يَضُرُّهُمْ مَنْ خَذَلَهُمْ وَلَا مَنْ خَالَفَهُمْ»

"A group of my *Ummah* will remain victorious upon the truth. They will not be harmed by those who forsake them or oppose them."[1]

They uphold the truth, resist falsehood, clarify the people's mistakes, expose misguidance, warn against innovations, and caution against those who promote deviation.

The greatest contribution of this group in serving the religion is their effort in critiquing the people of innovation, exposing their flaws, and clarifying the misguidance and innovations they bring—from the time of the Companions until today.

---

[1] Collected by Muslim in his *Sahih* (no. 1920), Abu Dawud in his *Sunan* (no. 4252), Al-Tirmidhi in his *Jami'* (no. 2229), and Ibn Majah in his *Sunan* (no. 10).

When Ibn 'Umar learned that some people in Iraq were diligently seeking knowledge but were denying Divine Decree, saying, "There is no predestination. Things happen as they do," did he remain silent? Did he hesitate, saying, "Maybe this or that"? Nay, he said, "Inform them I am free from them, and they are free from me. By Allah, if one of them were to spend gold equal to the size of Mount Uhud, it would not benefit them until they believe in Divine Decree."[1] Ibn 'Umar distanced himself from them because they introduced a major innovation into the religion of Allah, one that contradicts the Qur'an and *Sunnah*. Both the Qur'an and *Sunnah* are definitive sources of evidence. A Muslim cites evidence from these two Revelations to refute falsehood, whichever readily comes to mind. Here, Ibn 'Umar referred to the *hadith* of Jibril, where he came to the Prophet (ﷺ) and asked about Islam, *Iman*, and *Ihsan*. In this *hadith*, the Messenger (ﷺ) explained that *Iman* includes belief in Allah, His angels, His books, His messengers, the Last Day, and Divine Decree (good and bad). Ibn 'Umar recited this *hadith* in full, emphasizing that belief in predestination, its good and bad, is a fundamental pillar of *Iman*. Whoever denies predestination destroys one pillar of faith, and when this pillar collapses, *Iman* falls. For this reason, Ibn 'Umar freed himself from those individuals.

---

[1] Collected by Muslim in his *Sahih* (no. 8), Abu Dawud in his *Sunan* (no. 4695), Al-Tirmidhi in his *Jami'* (no. 2610), and Al-Nasa'i in his *Sunan* (no. 4990).

The *imams* who followed, from the generation of the *Tabi'un*, their followers, and onward to this day, have always clarified and corrected errors. Scholars, jurists, and commentators all made corrections. If someone made a mistake, they said, "He erred." If someone strayed in his interpretation (*tafsir*), they said, "He deviated," or "He innovated."

Many scholars critiqued Al-Zamakhshari's *tafsir*. They pointed out its errors, criticized it, and some even went as far as to burn it because it contained hidden innovations. Similarly, Al-Ghazali's *Ihya 'Ulum al-Din* was widely criticized by scholars. It included jurisprudence, *hadith*, *tafsir*, and *tasawwuf*. It also introduced philosophy, the concept of *Wahdat al-Wujud* (the unity of existence), and other misguidances and innovations. Some scholars burned this book, some critiqued it, and some even declared Al-Ghazali a disbeliever. No one objected, saying, "Why are you criticizing Al-Ghazali, Al-Razi, Al-Zamakhshari, or anyone else?"

Imams like Al-Daraqutni came after Al-Bukhari and Muslim and critiqued some of the *hadiths* in their collections. Scholars such as Abu 'Ali Al-Jayyani and others also examined the *Sahihayn* and pointed out certain weaknesses. However, in most cases, the correctness lies with the two *shaykhs*, yet no one got up in arms over these critiques. Why? Because these scholars respected the people's intellect, upheld the truth, and maintained a good opinion of others. Not everyone who

34

critiques a person is automatically accused of bad intentions, envy, or hatred, as is common nowadays.

People did not say, "These individuals are busy confronting the Jews, Christians, philosophers, and so on, so leave them alone," even when they were refuting the *Rafidah*. The *Mu'tazilah*, for instance, used to refute the *Rafidah*, the *Khawarij*, and others, but their own errors were not overlooked. Should we, because someone is rebutting the Jews and Christians, attribute their mistakes to Allah and claim that they are part of the religion, leading the *Ummah* astray? Or should we say, "As long as so-and-so is refuting the Jews and Christians, all of their errors are excused and included in the religion"? Meaning do we take one issue in the faith, add twenty more errors of the *Rafidah* to it, and attribute them to the religion of Allah? Is this acceptable? Is this how it should be? Is this how advice is given to Muslims? Is this how clarity is provided? If someone were to confront them with swords, march armies against them, and do whatever, yet made mistakes concerning the religion of Allah and went astray in it, we would say, "This is not from the religion. This is misguidance and innovation that cannot be attributed to Allah's *Din*."

Allah did not leave even the Prophet (ﷺ) and his Companions at Badr in their error. So, how can we ignore the errors of others and allow them to distort the religion of Allah or shake the foundations of Islam under the pretext of confronting communists? Let them confront them, and we pray that Allah rewards them, Allah willing. However, we cannot attribute their mistakes to Allah's religion or treat their errors as if they were unquestionable divine revelation. Even the *Mu'tazilah* did not take offense when critiqued, nor did the scholars of *Ahl al-Sunnah*. Sometimes, a *Mu'tazili* might be correct in critiquing a scholar from *Ahl Al-Sunnah*, though the truth is most often with *Ahl Al-Sunnah*. This ongoing [process of critique]—from the past to the present and continuing until the Day of Judgment—remains essential. Every person's words may be accepted or rejected. It is not the case that every statement is accepted or every statement is rejected. No, even scholars like Al-Shafi'i, Ahmad, Malik, Al-Thawri, and Al-Awza'i had their opinions accepted or rejected because they were not infallible. As Ibn Taymiyyah said, infallibility belongs only to the prophets. As for the truthful ones, martyrs, righteous people, and *imams*, they are all bound to make mistakes.

Al-Shafi'i himself said, "Look at my writings. Do not assume that everything in them is correct. Undoubtedly, they contain errors that contradict the Book of Allah or the *Sunnah* of Allah's Messenger (ﷺ). Whatever conflicts with either of them, take it and throw it away."

Take my books and read them, but I do not claim everything in them is correct. There are undoubtedly errors. I emphasize this. Once, someone said to me, "So-and-so wants to debate you." I replied, let him come quickly before I die so he can point out my mistakes. I urge you all to go and ask Salman and Safar[1] to gather my books, review them, and clarify the truth in them so that I can repent [from my errors] before my death. Criticism does not offend us. By Allah, we are happy with it. I hold each of you responsible for going to them with my books so that they may examine them. If anyone finds a mistake, I will say, 'May Allah reward you,' and send them gifts. If I am unable to do so, I will pray for them. By Allah, we are not afraid of criticism because we are not infallible. I seek Allah's forgiveness. Who are we to say, "We are not infallible"? This is something said about the Companions and the great *imams*. As for us—may Allah protect us—significant errors are to be expected from us.

I sincerely hope that they take my books and critique them: 'On page such-and-such, you said this, and it is wrong. Your reasoning is flawed from this angle and that angle. The *hadith* you cited was misused, and you misquoted this *hadith*.' Please, my brother, come forward. Why are you upset? Why are you

---

[1] **TN:** Here, the *Shaykh* is alluding to Safar Al-Hawali and Salman Al-Awdah, two figureheads of the neo-Kharijites. *Al-Allamah* Ahmad Al-Najmi said, "Indeed, these people, including Salman Al-Awdah are *takfiris* and those who incite the common people against the government. Their statements are recorded, documented, and well-known. It is incumbent upon them to repent to Allah from this," Ahmad b. Yahya Al-Najmi, audio recording, accessed December 10, 2024, https://youtube.com/shorts/MSj5f8fpxjA?si=F3O-gKMTFHrpDlZg..

teaching people blind fanaticism, arrogance, ignorance, and chaos? Why are you destroying young minds with this blind partisanship? Has there ever been a time when people showed fanaticism toward Al-Shafi'i or Malik like this? This kind of extreme partisanship is something we only know from the *Rafidah*, who elevate individuals to the level of prophets, making them beyond criticism. I hear some people say, "We welcome criticism and are happy to receive it," but by Allah, they cannot handle it. Criticism crushes them, and their followers fiercely defend them, asking, "Why are you criticizing him?" Therefore, we see that whenever we point out their mistakes, they never acknowledge or correct them—neither they nor their followers. It is as if our religion differs from theirs, as if we have a religion other than the one they know. My brother, do you not claim that you are upon the *Salafi* methodology and that you call to the Qur'an and *Sunnah*? What does it mean to call to them? It means to critique everyone's mistakes, not to collect your errors and label them as the Qur'an and *Sunnah*.

Your mistakes, along with those of others among the inexperienced and unlearned youth, have filled tapes and books with errors. Their writings draw heavily on the ideas of Sayyid Qutb, Al-Banna, and Al-Mawdudi, resulting in considerable misguidance and innovation. As a result, there are many inaccuracies. If they are sincere, they may unknowingly fall into these mistakes, thinking that Al-Mawdudi and Al-Banna are right, only to discover later that these figures are innovators and misguided. They discovered these individuals are people of desires through criticism from us or others. It is, therefore, impermissible to rely on their books, ideologies, or methodologies because they do not represent sound knowledge but the views of misguided individuals promoting innovations.

My brother, you grew up in a land of *tawhid* and *Sunnah* (i.e., Saudi Arabia), which Allah has blessed and distinguished. In this land, the banner of *tawhid* and *Sunnah* has been raised high, the light of Islam is clear, and innovations have been eradicated, with their proponents humiliated. This blessing from Allah must be appreciated, and you should dedicate yourself to this methodology and this great heritage and draw from it to present it to the *Ummah*. At the same time, this methodology is a one of truth. Even the *imams* and scholars who wrote and adhered to the correct methodology may have made mistakes. If Ibn Taymiyyah made an error, we would not accept it. The same applies to Ibn al-Qayyim, Ibn ʿAbd al-Wahhab, Ibn Baz, and others. If they made mistakes, we evaluate them against the Book of Allah, the *Sunnah* of the Messenger (صَلَّاللَّهُعَلَيْهِوَعَلَىآلِهِوَسَلَّم), and the *Salafi* methodology. We would point out the error, say, "Allah reward you," and move on—without criticism, insults, defamation, or revilement. Instead, we clarify that a specific statement conflicts with a particular principle or text, doing so with the utmost respect and courtesy. As *Shaykh al-Islam* Ibn Taymiyyah, Ibn Rajab, and others have said. We discuss their views with respect, civility, and good intentions, aiming only to clarify the truth.

Ibn Rajab has some excellent remarks on this topic, which we will read in future lessons, Allah willing. We will also study the words of Ibn Taymiyyah and Al-Nawawi on these matters, as they have made valuable contributions here.

Explanation of Some Passages from *The Difference Between Advice and Revilement*

[This is from] the book: *The Difference Between Advice and Revilement.*

When criticizing someone, you must adhere to truthfulness, honesty, and sincerity, to clarify the *haqq* and point out the error that contradicts it.

If this is your intention, it is an honorable aim and a noble act for which the entire *Ummah* should thank you. No one may accuse you of ill intent. However, if your intentions are found—through investigation and examination—to be driven by personal bias or desires, then people may speak about you.

Al-Hafiz Ibn Rajab said,

((الحمدُ لله رب العالمين، وصلاته وسلامه عَلَى إمام المتقين، وخاتم النبيين وآله وصحبه أجمعين، والتابعين لهم بإحسانٍ إلَى يوم الدين

أما بعد: فهذه كلماتٌ مختصرةٌ جامعةٌ في الفرق بين النصيحة والتعيير، فإنّهما يشتركان في أنّ كلاً منهما ذكر للإنسان بما يكره ذكره، وقد يشتبه الفرق بينهما عند كثير من الناس. والله الموفق للصواب.))

"Praise be to Allah, the Lord of all the worlds, and may His blessings and peace be upon the leader of the pious, the seal

41

of the prophets, and upon his family, companions, and all those who follow them with goodness until the Day of Judgment.

To proceed: These are brief and comprehensive words on the difference between advice and revilement. Both involve mentioning something about a person he dislikes, and the distinction between them may be unclear to many people. May Allah guide us to what is correct."[1]

Advice involves mentioning something about a person he dislikes. Is that incorrect? Similarly, revilement also involves mentioning something about a person he dislikes. This can sometimes cause confusion between advice and insult.

Revilement is pointing out a fault, is it not? Advice also involves pointing out a fault so that people are aware of it, especially if the person has an innovation or an error. However, the key difference is your intention. If you intend to seek Allah's Face, this is sincere advice.

Contrarily, this becomes shaming if you mention someone's fault to satisfy a grudge or out of personal animosity with no legitimate purpose. It is criticism driven by resentment, and it is sinful.

---

[1] 'Abd al-Rahman b. Ahmad b. Rajab Al-Hanbali, *Al-Farq Bayn Al-Nasihah wa Al-Ta'yir*, in *Majmu' Rasail Al-Hafidh Ibn Rajab Al-Hanbali*, vol. 2 (Cairo: Al-Faruq Al-Haditha, 1st ed., 1424 AH / 2003 CE), 403.

He then said,

«اعلم أن ذكر الإنسان بما يكره محرَّم، إذا كان المقصود منه مجرَّد الذم والعيب والنقص، فأمَّا إن كان فيه مصلحة لعامة المسلمين، أو خاصة لبعضهم، وكان المقصودُ منه تحصيلِ تلك المصلحةِ، فليس بمحرم، بل مندوب إِليه»

"Know that mentioning something about a person he dislikes is prohibited if the intent is merely to criticize, belittle, or point out his faults. However, if there is a benefit in doing so—whether for the general Muslims or a specific group—and the intention is to achieve that benefit, then it is not prohibited. It is encouraged."[1]

Rather, it is obligatory because Allah has commanded clarification. It is not merely encouraged.

Al-Hafiz Ibn Rajab said,

«و قد قرر علماء الحديث هذا في كتبهم في الجرح و التعديل و ذكروا الفَرق بين جَرح الرواة و بين الغِيبة.»

"The scholars of *hadith* have established this principle in their books on *Al-Jarh wa Al-Ta'dil* (criticism and praise of

---

[1] Ibn Rajab, *Al-Farq Bayn Al-Nasihah wa Al-Ta'yir*, 403.

narrators) and have clarified the difference between critiquing narrators and backbiting."[1]

Backbiting involves mentioning your brother in a way he dislikes, with a personal motive and without seeking Allah's pleasure, intending only to defame him. However, critiquing narrators is about safeguarding the religion of Allah. How else can we distinguish between authentic and weak narrations if no one evaluates the narrators? If no one critiques them, whether they are *Rafidis*, *Jahmis*, liars, or misinformers, would this not lead to the religion's ruin? Would this not result in the faith's corruption? Consider the volumes of books on fabricated traditions and the extensive works on hidden defects (*'ilal*) in *hadith*. What is their purpose? Their purpose is critiquing narrators, analyzing chains of transmission, and evaluating the texts to identify interpolations, broken chains, and other issues.

He said,

«وَ ذَكَرُوا الفَرْقَ بَيْنَ جَرْحِ الرُّوَاةِ وَ بَيْنَ الغِيبَةِ.»

"And they clarified the difference between critiquing narrators and backbiting."

Backbiting does not serve the religion. Rather, it may destroy it for trivial purposes. In contrast, critiquing narrators has

---

[1] Ibn Rajab, *Al-Farq Bayn Al-Nasihah wa Al-Ta'yir*, 403.

noble objectives: preserving and protecting the religion from being corrupted by mixing truth with falsehood. If we were to remain silent about narrators who are liars, accused of dishonesty, lacking in memory, or prone to serious errors, would the religion not be lost? However, Allah has preserved this faith through this criticism, evaluation, and distinction between reliable and unreliable transmitters. The benefits of this science are clear, and all praise is for Allah.

The *Sufis*, in their ignorance, wished to silence narrators and critics. If the scholars of *Jarh wa Ta'dil* and *hadith* criticism had surrendered to such pressures, the religion of Allah would have been lost. Yet Allah refuses except to complete His light, even if the innovators detest it.

Ibn Rajab said,

((ورُّدوا عَلَى من سَوَّى بينهما من المتعبدين وغيرهم ممن لا يَّتسع علمه.))

"They refuted those, including the worshippers and others with limited knowledge, who equated the two."[1]

These were the *Sufis* who objected to the scholars of *hadith*, accusing them of backbiting. The scholars of *hadith* responded, saying, "This is not backbiting. This is sincere advice and clarification." Of course, many people do not truly understand the Qur'an and *Sunnah*.

---

[1] Ibn Rajab, *Al-Farq Bayn Al-Nasihah wa Al-Ta'yir*, 403.

Those who follow the ways of the innovators and the *Sufis* in forbidding critique and accountability have adopted their approach, not that of *Ahl al-Sunnah*. By Allah, we wish they would critique us to point out our mistakes so we may repent from them before we die.

He then said,

‹‹ولا فرق بين الطعن في رواة ألفاظ الحديث والتمييز بين من تُقبل روايتُه منهم ومن لا تُقبل، وبين تبيين خطأ من أخطأ في فهم معاني الكتاب والسنة وتأوّل شيئًا منها عَلَى غير تأويله، وتمسَّك بما لا يتمسَّك به؛ ليحذر من الاقتداء به فيما أخطأ فيه، وقد أجمع العُلَماء عَلَى جواز ذلك أيضًا.

ولهذا تجد كتبهم المصنَّفة في أنواع العلوم الشرعية من التفسير، وشرح الحديث، والفقه، واختلاف العُلَماء وغير ذلك ممتلئة من المناظرات، وردوا من أقوال تضعَّف أقواله من أئمة السلف والخلف، من الصحابة والتابعين ومن بعدهم. ولم ينكر ذلك أحُد من أهل العِلْم، ولا أدعى فيه طعنًا عَلَى من ردَّ عليه قوله، ولا ذمًّا ولا نقصًا، اللهم إلا أن يكون المصنَّفُ يُفحش في الكلام، ويسيء الأدب في العبارة فيُنكر عليه فحاشتُه وإساءتُه دون أصل رده، ومخالفته إقامة الحجج الشرية، والأدلة المعتبرة.

وسبب ذلك أن علماء الدين كلهم مُجمعون عَلَى قصد إظهار الحق الَّذي بعث الله به رسوله – صلى الله عليه وسلم –، وأن يكون الدينُ كُله لله، وأن تكون كلمته هي العليا.››

46

"There is no difference between criticizing the narrators of *hadith* to determine whose narrations are accepted or rejected and clarifying the errors of those who misunderstand the meanings of the Qur'an and *Sunnah*, misinterpret them, or adhere to points that should not be followed. This clarification serves to warn people against following such errors. Scholars have unanimously agreed on the permissibility of this as well.

For this reason, we find many debates and refutations of weak opinions in their various books on Islamic sciences—such as *tafsir*, *hadith* commentaries, *fiqh*, and the discussions of scholarly disagreements. This includes opinions held by the *imams* of both earlier and later generations, including the Companions, the *Tabi'un*, and those who came after them. None of the scholars refrained from this, nor did they consider such refutations personal attacks, criticism, or belittlement of those whose views were refuted—unless a writer indulged in excessively harsh language or insulting words. In such cases, their harshness and poor manners were criticized, not the act of refutation itself, as long as the critique was based on sound evidence and legitimate arguments.

The reason for this is that all scholars of the religion are united in their aim to reveal the truth that Allah sent with

His Messenger (ﷺ), to ensure that the religion belongs entirely to Allah, and that His word is uppermost."[1]

He is saying there is no difference between critiquing narrators and pointing out someone's errors in religion, whether in jurisprudence, *hadith*, *tafsir*, Islamic principles, or any other field—or if they hold an innovation.

Some people claim, "This critique is only for narrators to preserve the *Sunnah* of the Messenger of Allah." We respond to them, What about the beliefs of the Muslims? If people come to distort and undermine them, should they not be criticized?

Should we not critique the *Jahmiyyah*? Should we not critique the *Rafidah*, who have no connection to narration, but bring beliefs that contradict and oppose Islam? Should we remain silent about them? What about *Sufis* who promote *Hulul* (incarnation), *Wahdat Al-Wujud* (unity of existence), dancing, chants, innovations, and misguided forms of remembrance? Even though they are not narrators, we must critique them.

Yusuf Al-Qaradawi was once asked whether the *Ash'aris* are from *Ahl al-Sunnah*, and he erupted like a volcano: "They say the *Ash'aris* are not from *Ahl al-Sunnah*! Where are we going with this? The *Ash'aris* are everywhere! The world's universities are almost all *Ash'ari*. Al-Azhar, which has served Islam for a

---

[1] Ibn Rajab, *Al-Farq Bayn Al-Nasihah wa Al-Ta'yir*, 403-404.

thousand years, is *Ash'ari*. Al-Zaytuna, Al-Qarawiyyin, Deoband—all of them are *Ash'ari*!"[1]

I do not know the cause of this. Perhaps there were *Salafi* youth they wanted to brainwash. These poor individuals were forced to sit before this volcanic eruption. What else could they say?

The *Ash'ari* creed today aligns with the *Jahmiyyah* in negating Allah's attributes. This is why *Shaykh al-Islam* Ibn Taymiyyah authored several refutations against them, including *Talbisat Al-Jahmiyyah*. Who are the *Jahmiyyah* mentioned by Ibn Taymiyyah? He says they are none other than the *Ash'aris*—such as Al-Razi and others. When he recounts the debates between him and the *Ash'aris* in his time, he refers to them as "the *Jahmiyyah*," repeatedly using this term. He classified both the Ash'aris and the *Mu'tazilah* as branches of the *Jahmiyyah*. He further said about the *Ash'aris*, "Whoever among them adheres to the teachings found in *Al-Ibanah* by Abu al-Hasan al-Ash'ari, which he authored at the end of his life and did not contradict, then whoever follows what is in *Al-Ibanah* is from *Ahl al-Sunnah*—on the condition they do not call themselves Al-

---

[1] Participating with him in this seminar were: Al-Ghanushi and Fahmy Huwaydi. The essence of Al-Ghanushi's talk was to criticize those who speak against the *Shiites*, while Huwaydi's intention was to emphasize benefiting from the *Batiniyyah* so that their energies are not wasted and Islam does not miss out on their contributions.

This, by Allah, marks the ultimate plotting against Islam and its followers. Let us not forget the Muslim Brotherhood's interfaith conferences.

Ash'ari, as such an ascription causes harm and misleads people."[1]

Most of the *Salaf's* criticisms against the *Jahmiyyah* were directed at their denial of Allah's Loftiness. They claimed Allah is neither inside the creation nor outside it, neither above nor below nor in any position at all. By this, they rejected hundreds of texts from the Qur'an and *Sunnah*. Alternatively, they would say, "Allah is in every place."

'Abd Allah b. Al-Mubarak said, "We can repeat the words of the Jews and Christians and others, but we cannot repeat the words of the *Jahmiyyah*." This refers to statements like, "Allah is neither above nor below" or "Allah is in every place," accompanied by their denial of this great attribute and distortion of the many texts in the Qur'an and *Sunnah* that affirm it.

These reservations, precautions, and guidelines are for when we speak about the *imams* of the religion. We must address them with respect, good manners, and sincerity, seeking Allah's Face. Critiquing their words to defame, discredit, or attack them is impermissible. This is never allowed. As for the people of falsehood and innovation, their scandals must be exposed, and such caution does not apply to them. The same applies to ignorant individuals who imitate scholars but are not truly knowledgeable. Their ignorance and misguidance must be uncovered.

---

[1] *Majmu' Al-Fatawa* (6/359)

After offering wise words about addressing the mistakes of scholars with respect, Ibn Rajab said,

«وهذا كُلّه في حقّ العُلماء المُقتدى بهم في الدِّين، فأمّا أهل البدع والضلالة ومن تشبه بالعُلماء وليس منهم، فيجوزُ بيانُ جهلهم، وإظهار عيوبهم تحذيرًا من الاقتداء بهم. وليس كلامنا الآن في هذا القبيل، والله أعلم.»

All of this applies to scholars who are followed in matters of religion. As for the people of innovation and misguidance, or those who imitate scholars while not being from them, it is permissible to expose their ignorance and reveal their faults to warn others against following them. However, our discussion here does not concern this category. And Allah knows best.[1]

He then said:

«وَمَنْ عُرف منه أنه أُراد بردّه عَلَى العُلماء النصيحةَ لله ورسوله، فإنه يجب أن يُعامل بالإكرام والاحترام والتعظيم كسائر أئمّة المسلمين الذين سبق ذكرهم وأمثالهم ومن اتبعهم بإحسان.

ومن عرف أنه أُراد بردّه عليهم التنقص والذم، وإظهار العيب، فإنه يستحقُّ أن يُقابل بالعُقوبة ليرتدع هو ونظراؤه عن هذه الرذائل المحرمة.»

Whoever is known to refute scholars intending to offer sincere advice for the sake of Allah and His Messenger (صَلَّىٰ ٱللَّهُ عَلَيْهِ وَعَلَىٰ آلِهِ وَسَلَّمَ) should be treated with honor, respect, and

---

[1] Ibn Rajab, *Al-Farq Bayn Al-Nasihah wa Al-Ta'yir*, 407.

esteem, just like the other *imams* of Islam previously mentioned and their likes, along with those who follow them in goodness.

However, whoever is known to refute scholars intending to belittle, criticize, or expose faults deserves to be punished to deter them and others like them from such prohibited, disgraceful behavior."[1]

This latter behavior is currently practiced by the opponents of *Ahl al-Sunnah wa Al-Jama ah*, particularly the partisans who actively oppose the methodology of the *Salaf* and support the people of innovation and desires.

As for the scholars and the people of guidance, by Allah, they rejoice in the clarification of truth. If someone points out one of their errors and explains it to the people, they are pleased. This is why we see that the students of these *imams* do not hesitate to clarify their teachers' mistakes or to differ with them on opinions where they believe an error occurred. They firmly believe that their *imams* would approve of this and would never want people to follow their missteps as acts of worship, nor would they ever accept that their mistakes be attributed to Allah. They would never allow such a thing because of their sincerity, truthfulness, and commitment to advising for the sake of Allah, His Messenger (ﷺ), His Book, the leaders of the Muslims, and the common folk—may Allah be

---

[1] Ibn Rajab, *Al-Farq Bayn Al-Nasihah wa Al-Ta'yir*, 408.

52

pleased with them. However, the people of desires refuse to admit anyone's mistakes, whether the person is alive or deceased, regardless of their deviation or misguidance. They cannot bear criticism, and so they stubbornly resist. Even when *Ahl al-Sunnah* and the people of truth clarify their errors and misguidance on specific issues, providing clear evidence, they continue to cling to their falsehood. They gather people around these deviant ideas, rallying them to support their misguided beliefs, showing no fear of the grave consequences of their actions or Allah's severe punishment. They lead people astray and divert them from the path of guidance because their hearts have been turned upside down—may Allah protect us—and their desires have overcome them. As the Messenger of Allah (صَلَّاللَهُ عَلَيْهِ وَعَلَى آلِهِ وَسَلَّمَ) described them,

$$ ((تَتَجَلَّى بِهِمُ الْأَهْوَاءُ كَمَا يَتَجَلَّى الْكَلْبُ بِصَاحِبِهِ)) $$

"Their desires run through them like rabies through its victim."[1]

For this reason, the *Salaf* referred to them as "people of desires" and called the people of truth "*Ahl Al-Sunnah wa Al-Jama'ah*." They also referred to them as "people of knowledge" and "people of hadith," honoring them with noble titles. In contrast, they called the others "people of misguidance," "people of innovation," and "people of desires," such as the

---

[1] Collected by Ibn Abu 'Asim in *Al-Sunnah* (nos. 1 and 2) and authenticated by Al-Albani based on supporting narrations.

Jahmiyyah, Mu'tazilah, Qadariyyah, Murji'ah, Khawarij, Rafidah, and others. They are all grouped as "people of desires" because those who fall into error due to ignorance and personal desires do not retract their mistakes. In contrast, the people of truth and knowledge, those who call to Allah, are motivated to spread and teach knowledge only out of hope for the great reward Allah has prepared for the inheritors of the prophets. They inherit the responsibility of clarifying the truth and calling to it. They are deeply fearful of making mistakes. If someone points out their errors, they rejoice and encourage them to do so.

The Qur'an would sometimes come with verses that aligned with the opinions of 'Umar. Did the Messenger of Allah (صَلَّى ٱللَّهُ عَلَيْهِ وَعَلَىٰ آلِهِ وَسَلَّمَ) get upset? Did he regret it? Did he feel pained and say, "Allah supports 'Umar while I am left out"? I seek Allah's forgiveness! The same applies to Abu Bakr and the rest of the Companions. They were happy when someone clarified their mistakes.

Similarly, the *imams* of the religion—as we have mentioned repeatedly—welcomed correction. This was a reflection on the previous lesson from this book. Tonight, we want to read some statements from the scholars that show that criticism, driven by a proper Islamic purpose, is necessary and may even be obligatory. This is because it benefits the *Ummah*, offers sincere advice, strengthens them in truth and goodness, and protects them from evil, misguidance, and desires. We will take a section from *Riyad al-Salihin* and perhaps read some of its chapters, Allah willing. I encourage you to read this book, as it is beneficial.

Permissible Cases of Backbiting

Al-Nawawi said in *Riyad al-Salihin*:

Chapter: What is Permissible in Backbiting

‹‹اعْلَمْ أَنَّ الْغِيبَةَ تُبَاحُ لِغَرَضٍ صَحِيحٍ شَرْعِيٍّ لاَ يُمْكِنُ الْوُصُولُ إِلَيْهِ إِلاَّ بِهَا, وَهُوَ سِتَّةُ أَسْبَابٍ››

"Know that backbiting is permitted for a valid, legitimate Islamic purpose that cannot be achieved except through it, and this applies to six cases."[1]

He called it backbiting and said, "It is permissible," though it is not truly backbiting but advice. He used the term leniently because some perceive it as backbiting. Even if it were considered backbiting, it would be permissible—rather, obligatory—as he stated.

‹‹الأَوَّلُ: التَّظَلُّمُ, فَيَجُوزُ لِلمَظْلُومِ أَنْ يَتَظَلَّمَ إِلَى السُّلْطَانِ وَالقَاضِي وَغَيرِهِمَا مِمَّنْ لَهُ وِلاَيَةٌ, أَوْ قُدْرَةٌ عَلَى إِنصَافِهِ مِنْ ظَالِمِهِ, فَيقول: ظَلَمَنِي فُلاَنٌ بِكَذَا.››

First, it is allowed for an oppressed person to complain to the ruler, a judge, or others in authority to grant him justice

---

[1] Yahya b. Sharaf al-Nawawī, *Riyadh Al-Salihin* (Beirut, Lebanon: *Mu'assasat al-Risalah*, 3rd ed., 1419 AH / 1998 CE), 432.

from his oppressor. For example, he may say, "So-and-so wronged me in such-and-such matter."[1]

Allah said,

$$﴿ لَّا يُحِبُّ ٱللَّهُ ٱلْجَهْرَ بِٱلسُّوٓءِ مِنَ ٱلْقَوْلِ إِلَّا مَن ظُلِمَ ﴾$$

"Allah does not like public mention of evil except by one who has been wronged" (*Al-Nisa*: 4:148).

This verse is evidence that one who has been wronged may speak out about the wrongdoing, such as saying, "So-and-so wronged me," bringing the case to court, filing a claim, and providing witnesses against [the oppressor], and so on.

«الثَّانِي: الاسْتِعَانَةُ عَلَى تَغْيِيرِ الْمُنْكَرِ, وَرَدِّ الْعَاصِي إِلَى الصَّوَابِ, فَيَقُولُ لِمَنْ يَرْجُو قُدْرَتَهُ عَلَى إِزَالَةِ الْمُنْكَرِ: ׳فُلَانٌ يَعْمَلُ كَذَا, فَازْجُرْهُ عَنْهُ׳ وَنَحْوَ ذَلِكَ وَيَكُونُ مَقْصُودُهُ التَّوَصُّلَ إِلَى إِزَالَةِ الْمُنْكَرِ, فَإِنْ لَمْ يَقْصِدْ ذَلِكَ كَانَ حَرَامًا.»

"Second, seeking help to remove wrongdoing and guide a sinner back to the correct path is permissible. For instance, one may say to someone capable of addressing the wrongdoing, "So-and-so is doing such-and-such, so prevent him," or something similar to remove the harm. However,

---

[1] Al-Nawawi, *Riyadh al-Salihin*, 432.

if the purpose is not to remove the evil but to harm the individual or seek revenge, then it is prohibited."[1]

In other words, if the advice is given to seek revenge or harm the person in question, it is sinful. If someone commits a wrongdoing and does not stop when admonished, you may seek the help of authorities, such as the ruler, a judge, or someone who can deter and prevent him from his transgressions. For example, if someone is drinking alcohol, committing adultery, stealing, spreading innovations, harming people, or committing highway robbery, you can report him and escalate the matter to someone who can stop his oppression. Your intent should be to please Allah and eradicate the evil He has forbidden. The Prophet (ﷺ) said,

﴿مَنْ رَأَى مِنْكُمْ مُنْكَرًا فَلْيُغَيِّرْهُ بِيَدِهِ فَإِنْ لَمْ يَسْتَطِعْ فَبِلِسَانِهِ فَإِنْ لَمْ يَسْتَطِعْ فَبِقَلْبِهِ وَذَلِكَ أَضْعَفُ الْإِيمَانِ.﴾

"Whoever among you sees an evil, let him change it with his hand; if he is unable, then with his tongue; and if he is unable, then with his heart, and that is the weakest of faith."[2]

---

[1] Al-Nawawi, *Riyadh al-Salihin*, 432.

[2] Collected by Al-Bukhari in *Kitab al-Jumu'ah* (114), Muslim in *Kitab al-Iman* (49), Al-Tirmidhi in *Kitab al-Fitan* (2172), Abu Dawud in *Kitab al-Salah* (1140), and others.

This involves striving to remove the evil, either personally—if one is able—or through someone else. Where one cannot remove the evil himself, he may resort to someone in authority who has the power to remove it. This is permissible and may even become obligatory, as we must work towards eliminating evil.

«الثَّالِثُ: الاسْتِفْتَاءُ, فَيَقُولُ لِلْمُفْتِي: ظَلَمَنِي أَبِي , أَوْ أَخِي , أَوْ زَوْجِي , أَوْ فُلَانٌ بِكَذَا , فَهَلْ لَهُ ذَلِكَ؟ وَمَا طَرِيقِي فِي الخَلَاصِ مِنْهُ , وَتَحْصِيلِ حَقِّي , وَدَفْعِ الظُّلْمِ؟ وَنَحْوُ ذَلِكَ , فَهَذَا جَائِزٌ لِلْحَاجَةِ , ولَكِنَّ الأَحْوَطَ والأَفْضَلَ أَنْ يقول: مَا تقولُ فِي رَجُلٍ أَوْ شَخْصٍ , أَوْ زَوْجٍ , كَانَ مِنْ أَمْرِهِ كَذَا , فَإِنَّهُ يَحْصُلُ بِهِ الغَرَضُ مِنْ غَيْرِ تَعْيِينٍ وَمَعَ ذَلِكَ , فَالتَّعْيِينُ جَائِزٌ كما سَنَذْكُرُه فِي حَدِيثِ هِنْدٍ إِنْ شَاءَ الله تَعَالَى.»

"Third, it is permissible for someone to seek a verdict from a *mufti*: 'My father, brother, husband, or so-and-so wronged me in such-and-such a matter. Is this permissible for them? How can I resolve this, reclaim my rights, and repel this injustice?' This is allowed out of necessity. However, it is safer and better to say, 'What do you say about a man, a person, or a spouse who did such and such?' This achieves the intended purpose without specifying the individual. Nonetheless, specifying the person is also permissible, as will be explained in the *hadith* of Hind, Allah willing."[1]

---

[1] Al-Nawawi, *Riyadh al-Salihin*, 432.

The evidence for this is the incident where Hind bint 'Utbah came to the Prophet (ﷺ) and said, "O Messenger of Allah, Abu Sufyan is a miserly man." In another narration, she said, "He does not give me and my children enough to suffice us. Is it permissible for me to take from his wealth what is sufficient for me and my children?" The Prophet (ﷺ) said, "Take what reasonably suffices you and your children."[1]

From this, the scholars derived the permissibility of complaining to those in authority or someone capable of removing oppression.

The key point is that the Messenger of Allah (ﷺ) approved Hind's statement. He did not say, "This is backbiting," or, "Abu Sufyan is a great man, a Muslim, a prominent figure of Quraysh. Why are you speaking about him in this way? Why are you accusing him of being miserly?" The Prophet (ﷺ) did not object to her words but approved of her complaint and permitted her to take from his wealth what was sufficient for her and her children.

From this, the scholars of Islam derived evidence that it is permissible for someone seeking a *fatwa*—or someone complaining of an injustice—to present their case. He may say to a *mufti*, judge, or leader, "What is your opinion about a man who does such-and-such to his wife, does such-and-such to his

---

[1] Collected by Al-Bukhari in *Kitab al-Nafaqat* (5364), Muslim in *Kitab al-Aqdiyah* (1714), Abu Dawud in *Kitab al-Buyu* (3532), *Al-Nasa i in Kitab Adab al-Qada* (5403), and others.

children, does not spend on them, or does not fulfill their rights to food, clothing, and other necessities? Is it permissible for us to take from his wealth, even without his consent, what suffices his children and dependents?" Here, the authority would not consider this backbiting but instead respond, "Yes, it is permissible." Moreover, the authority may summon the man, compel him to fulfill his duties, and provide the necessary rights to his wife, family, and dependents.

((الرَّابِعُ: تَحْذِيرُ المُسْلِمِينَ مِنَ الشَّرِّ وَنَصِيحَتُهُمْ.))

"Fourth, warning Muslims against harm and advising them"[1]

This is permissible. For example, we warn Muslims about a sinful person or an innovator. Similarly, if someone gives false testimony or his testimony is invalid for any reason, and there is a flaw in his credibility, we clarify this flaw. This serves as sincere advice to the Muslims and helps protect them from harm.

He then said,

((مِنْهَا: جَوْحُ المَجْرُوحِينَ مِنَ الرُّوَاةِ وَالشُّهُودِ.))

"This includes critiquing discredited narrators and witnesses."[2]

---

[1] Al-Nawawi, *Riyadh al-Salihin*, 432.
[2] Al-Nawawi, *Riyadh al-Salihin*, 432.

If a narrator has a flaw—whether in integrity, accuracy, or is unknown, weak, accused of lying, or *mukhtalit*—it is permissible to clarify this when he says, "The Messenger of Allah said." Any flaw in his trustworthiness or precision must be addressed, especially if he narrates hadiths from the Messenger of Allah (ﷺ). It is essential to highlight any flaws in his accuracy, integrity, or reliability, regardless of who he is. The same applies to witnesses. If a witness makes a mistake in his testimony, lacks accuracy, or lies, we must critique him. We say, "So-and-so made a mistake in his testimony"—if he is known to be truthful. But if he made an error, we clarify he erred in his testimony and was inaccurate. We clarify his lie or fabrication if he gave false testimony or lied. This includes explaining his error or deliberate falsehood. Doing so is permissible by the consensus of the Muslims. Rather, it is obligatory. Al-Nawawi said,

«وَذَلِكَ جَائِزٌ بِإِجْمَاعِ الْمُسْلِمِينَ, بَلْ وَاجِبٌ لِلْحَاجَةِ.»

"It is not just permissible but obligatory when necessary."[1]

He clarifies it is permissible and, when necessary, obligatory, regardless of who the narrator or witness may be.

As for mentioning both the good and bad qualities of someone on every occasion, this is something we have only heard of in our times. It is a fabricated and contrived approach designed

---

[1] Al-Nawawi, *Riyadh al-Salihin*, 432.

to protect innovations and their proponents. This is its purpose, and it was not known to the *Salaf*. Let me say that if someone is writing people's biographies, he may include all aspects of their lives—good and bad—because he is relating history and narratives. However, if the purpose is to critique a person and warn against his innovation, misguidance, evil, or sinfulness, it suffices to highlight errors. If someone wants to document the history of a people, a nation, or an individual, he includes everything related to him—the good and the bad— whether it is a Muslim, a Jew, a Christian. Even when they tell the story of *Shaytan*, some say, "He was among the angels, then Allah transformed him into *Shaytan*." This is how they relate it.[1]

If you are recording history, there is no harm in mentioning both the good and bad qualities of people, whether they are Muslims or disbelievers. Even Pharaoh, when his biography is written, you find both good and bad mentioned about him. I remember reading when I was young that Qarun, one of Pharaoh's officials, went around collecting taxes and levies from the people of Egypt. He amassed a fortune so vast it seemed endless.

"Where did you get all this wealth?" Pharaoh asked him.

---

[1] *Al-Allamah* Ibn Baz said, "*Shaykh al-Islam* Ibn Taymiyyah and a group of scholars hold that Iblis is from the *jinn* and their progenitor, that Allah created him from smokeless fire, and he is not from the angels. However, he was engaged in worship in their company in the heavens. When he became arrogant, he was expelled and cursed. May Allah protect us," 'Abd Al-Aziz b. Baz, accessed December 9, 2024, www.binbaz.org.

"I collected it from taxes and other revenues," Qarun replied.

"It is not fitting for a lord to take from his servants. Return this wealth to its rightful owners."

We mention this as one of Pharaoh's good deeds. If you are a historian, document everything, good and bad. However, suppose you are a critic guiding and warning people against the harm of a book, a person, or a group or against their innovations and misguidance. Then, mentioning only what is necessary for critique suffices. There is no need to include their good qualities. But because of their ignorance, foolishness, and unbridled desires, some insist you cannot criticize a person or a book unless you mention their good and bad qualities. Otherwise, they accuse you of being unjust and dishonest. Where is this [principle] found? By applying this methodology, we discredit the *Salaf* and undermine their integrity from first to last. This approach would destroy Islam entirely.

So, shall we then dismiss Ahmad, Al-Bukhari, Al-Shafi'i, Ibn Ma'in, Yahya b. Sa'id Al-Qattan, and other *imams* of *Al-Jarh wa Al-Ta'dil*, such as Al-Daraqutni and Ibn Hibban, because of this methodology? Similarly, we would have to dismiss the *imams* of creed who criticized the *Jahmiyyah*, *Mu'tazilah*, and *Khawarij*, along with their leaders and beliefs, both individually and collectively. We would end up dismissing all the *imams* of *Ahl al-Sunnah*, erasing their legacy, and making them irrelevant. This would leave us with the people of innovation, misguidance, and deviation. This is a dangerous and corrupt methodology. May Allah protect us. Its proponents never

64

intended to benefit Islam or the Muslims. Their goal was to shield the people of innovation. This approach poses a serious threat to Islam and its *imams*, as it is entirely focused on defending the people of innovation.

For example, if I critique *Ihya Ulum al-Din* by Al-Ghazali and say, "It contains the concept of *Wahdat al-Wujud* (unity of existence), fabricated *hadiths*, and other issues," that is sufficient. By doing so, I have warned people about it, and I am not obligated to list both its merits and flaws—not at all—according to the consensus of the Muslims. Those who adopt this approach go against that consensus, putting Islam at hazard. Their methodology undermines the *imams* of Islam, subjecting them to unjust criticism and defamation. This flawed approach does not seek Allah's pleasure or sincere advice for Muslims. Instead, it defends the people of innovation and their books, which are filled with misguidance, superstitions, and deviations from the true path of Allah.

Al-Nawawi said,

((ومنها: المُشاوَرَة في 'مُصاهَرَة إِنْسانٍ, أو 'مُشاوَكِتِهِ, أو إِيداعِهِ, أو معامِلَتهِ, أو غير ذَلِكَ, أو 'مُجاوَرَتِه.))

"This also includes seeking advice regarding marrying into a family, partnering with someone, entrusting him with

65

something, conducting business with him, or living near him."[1]

For example, if you consider allowing someone to marry into your family and want to assess his suitability, you might go to someone who knows the person well and whom you trust. You would ask, "What is your opinion of so-and-so? He has come seeking to marry my sister, but I do not know him. Please advise me." If the person has faults, the advisor should mention them, such as, "He is stingy," or "He is abusive toward women," or "He frequently divorces," or "He is a liar." Any flaw that makes him unsuitable for marriage should be disclosed, as marriage involves close bonds. You must reveal such flaws, and it is impermissible to withhold any information. Additionally, you do not have to mention his good qualities, as this situation requires warning and sincere advice.

Similarly, if someone seeks to partner with another in business or trade—whether in commerce, agriculture, or another field—and asks, "What do you think of so-and-so?" the advisor might respond, "My brother, I have dealt with him, and I do not think he is suitable for partnership. He is dishonest, negligent, careless," or any other flaw. The advisor must disclose these issues, even if it is just one flaw. Failing to do so would make him a betrayer, not a sincere advisor.

---

[1] Al-Nawawi, *Riyadh al-Salihin*, 432.

Likewise, if someone intends to entrust his money or belongings to another, the advisor must verify the person's trustworthiness. For instance, he might say, "He is trustworthy," or "He is not trustworthy and has such-and-such issues."

Al-Nawawi said,

«ومنها: إِذَا رَأَى مُتَفَقِّهاً يَتَرَدَّدُ إِلَى مُبْتَدِعٍ, أَوْ فَاسِقٍ يَأْخُذُ عَنْهُ الْعِلْمَ, وَخَافَ أَنْ يَتَضَرَّرَ الْمُتَفَقِّهُ بِذَلِكَ, فَعَلَيْهِ نَصِيحَتُهُ بِبَيَانِ حَالِهِ, بِشَرْطِ أَنْ يَقْصِدَ النَّصِيحَةَ.»

"This also includes the case where one sees a student of knowledge frequently associating with an innovator or a sinner to learn from him and fears that this may harm the student. In such a situation, he must advise the student by clarifying that person's reality, provided that the intention is sincere advice."[1]

This is essential in every situation, as the intention must be sincere. He added,

«وَهَذَا مِمَّا يُغْلَطُ فِيهِ. وَقَدْ يَحْمِلُ الْمُتَكَلِّمَ بِذَلِكَ الْحَسَدُ وَيُلَبِّسُ الشَّيطان عَلَيْهِ ذَلِكَ.»

"This is one of the common mistakes people make. The speaker may be driven by envy, and *Shaytan* may deceive him in this matter."[2]

---

[1] Al-Nawawi, *Riyadh al-Salihin*, 432.
[2] Al-Nawawi, *Riyadh al-Salihin*, 432.

This means a scholar may not be an innovator or a sinner, but envy drives [the speaker] to accuse him of sin or innovation out of jealousy. This is forbidden, unjust, and oppressive. However, if the person in question is indeed an innovator or a sinner, and there is genuine concern that the student may adopt his innovations or be influenced by his immoral behavior, it becomes obligatory to offer sincere advice for the sake of Allah. The purpose must be to protect the student from harm, as [Al-Nawawi] stated.

He then said,

«وَمِنْهَا: أَنْ يَكُونَ لَهُ وِلَايَةٌ لَا يَقُومُ بِهَا عَلَى وَجْهِهَا.»

"This also includes when someone is in a position of authority but does not fulfill it properly..."[1]

This could be a leader, judge, or similar role.

«إِمَّا بِأَنْ لَايكُونَ صَالِحًا لَهَا، وِإِمَّا بِأَنْ يَكُونَ فَاسِقًا, أَوْ مُغَفَّلًا, وَنَحْوَ ذَلِكَ فَيَجِبُ ذِكْرُ ذَلِكَ.»

"...because they are unfit for it, sinful, negligent, or something of the sort. Here, it is obligatory to mention it."[2]

---

[1] Al-Nawawi, *Riyadh al-Salihin*, 432.
Two matters remain among those where backbiting is permissible:
[1] The one who openly commits sins.
[2] Identification, such as calling someone "the blind" or "the lame."
[2] Al-Nawawi, *Riyadh al-Salihin*, 432.

This applies to someone who has taken on a significant position affecting the interests or well-being of the Muslims. If he is not qualified, you must inform his superiors or someone capable of removing him and replacing him with someone more suitable for the Muslims. You must go to this authority and say, "So-and-so is not fit for this position."

If the judge is unjust or ignorant, one should say, "This person is not fit because he is ignorant and unjust." Similarly, if it is a leader, state, "This leader is unjust, ignorant, or unfit for his role," so that people can be relieved from his harm and someone more beneficial for the Muslims—someone who can better safeguard their wealth, lives, and honor—can be appointed in his place. Positions like these involve serious responsibilities where people's wealth, lives, and honor may be at risk. Such an unjust person might shed blood wrongfully, violate people's honor, or commit other harmful acts against Muslims. Therefore, anyone who knows about such flaws and deficiencies in a person must report him to his superiors— whether it is the ruler or someone else in a position to remove them—and recommend a replacement. This is necessary to protect people from harm and allow them to live safely, regarding their lives, wealth, and honor.

This advice should be taken to the appropriate authority for action. It is not suitable to stand on a *minbar* and deliver sermons in the *jahili* manner that is common today. As has happened with those who claim to enjoin good and forbid evil yet publicly criticize and attack the rulers—such as the Rightly

Guided Caliph 'Uthman. They slander him, and most of their statements are lies and fabrications.

Likewise, the people of *fitnah* today rely heavily on lies, fabrications, and exaggerations, turning molehills into mountains. Much of what they claim is entirely fabricated and baseless. This is their way.

As for those speaking about the Sudanese government, it is entirely about the innovations, misguidance, distortion of Islam, and its opposition to the truth and its followers. This includes the Sudanese government's sympathy toward the *Rafidah*, its relationships with Jews and Christians, its encouragement of grave worship, and its promotion of vices and misguidance. People must be warned because our youth are deceived by impostors who glorify Sudan and Afghanistan, falsely claiming them to be Islamic states and foundations for an Islamic caliphate. Yet, they are among the furthest nations from the religion of Allah. We cannot continue to dwell on these issues and fantasies that captivate so many youths. They say, "An Islamic state will arise in Afghanistan" or "The Islamic caliphate will emerge from Sudan." All of this is an empty delusion. What is built on corruption can only produce corruption, and what is built on falsehood can only produce falsehood.

These nations were established on falsehood, innovation, and misguidance. Afghanistan, for example, took Kabul with the support of communist forces.

Second, disputes and struggles erupted among them simply for the sake of power, not for the sake of the *Ummah*, Islam, or ruling according to what Allah has revealed. None of these noble objectives were their concern. It was only about who would take the seat of power, command the people, and control their lives, property, and blood. Both sides sought to take leadership. This led to massacres, and both sides allied with the communists. Both factions became deeply involved and allied with communists, *Batiniyyah*, *Rafidah*, secularists, and people from all other sects and beliefs. Can any good be expected to emerge from such conditions and such governments?[1]

The detractors among us incite the people against an Islamic state that has flaws, but they never address or speak truthfully about these facts. Why is that? Because they have partisan ties. These connections and affiliations between them and the governments of Sudan and Afghanistan silence their tongues and prevent them from speaking the truth.

Both a believer and a disbeliever may speak the truth, but these individuals cannot bring themselves to do so. Why? Because of their partisan links to these propagandists and agitators and to these deviant rulers who are far removed from the beliefs of Islam, the *Sunnah* of the Messenger of Allah (ﷺ), and the methodology of the *Salaf*. If a hint of the *Salafi* methodology or the Qur'an and *Sunnah* crosses their minds, their response is to attack its followers. That means turning to

---

[1] This was said during the time when Afghanistan was ruled by an *Ikhwani* party, which was being challenged for power by another *Ikhwani* party.

the people of Kunar[1] and slaughtering them or targeting the *masajid* of *Ansar al-Sunnah* in Sudan and seizing control of them. Meanwhile, all you see are alliances with the opponents of Allah, such as the *Rafidah* and Christians. Is remaining silent about "The Interfaith Summit" permissible?

A nation that has carried the banner of Islam for fifty years has declared to the entire *Ummah* that it will establish Allah's legislation. However, upon establishing this state, it began to sympathize with the *Rafidah* and Christians. It started visiting these Christian nations, flattering them, and claiming they were brothers who shared many religious principles and were more capable of implementing democracy. Is remaining silent in the face of such deceit and distortion permissible? Every day, graves are being built, and the authorities of this so-called Islamic state, which many ignorant people pin their hopes on as the foundation of the Islamic caliphate, hold celebrations over them. And one need not even mention the events taking place in Afghanistan. May Allah protect us.

Do you see a difference between a state founded on the *tawhid* of Allah and the *Sunnah* of His Messenger (ﷺ), where the *Sunnah* is upheld, innovations are suppressed, truth is honored, and its methodology follows the way of the predecessors—even if it has its sins and shortcomings—and states that only want to fight this?

---

[1] A province in northeastern Afghanistan, bordering Pakistan and the Hindu Kush mountains.

Can anyone now convince the Sudanese state to introduce *Kitab Al-Tawhid* or *The Three Fundamental Principles* into their schools? Who can persuade Burhani, Hikmatyar, or Ahmad Shah Mas'ud, to introduce *The Three Fundamental Principles* into the schools of Afghanistan?

Before they established their state and became arrogant, some generous people printed thousands of copies of *The Three Fundamental Principles* and other books for them. They presented these copies to the *Sayaf* office as a gift for students. A report stated that the two books were well-written but contradicted their beliefs. As a result, they refused to accept them. This generous benefactor was forced to take back his books and deliver them to the schools of Jamil Al-Rahman. They eagerly accepted them because these books aligned with their beliefs, religion, and methodology. Praise be to Allah. However, Hikmatyar did not accept this at all. Instead, he slaughtered those who upheld tawhid, followed the Sunnah, and applied Allah's legislation. This is the difference between the two, my brothers. May Allah bless you.

Despite its mistakes, a country established on the *Sunnah* keeps its doors open to those who wish to offer advice. It says, "Advise us. Write to us." They do not imprison anyone who writes or approaches them with observations. However, by Allah, no one would accept public defamation, not even a rightly guided Caliph. Such calumny is never acceptable. The sincere advisors of the past would approach the caliphs under cover of darkness and in private to offer their counsel. For example, Usamah b. Zayd and others would go to 'Uthman and speak to him privately. Meanwhile, the people of evil and discord would outwardly pretend to enjoin good and forbid evil, standing on *manabir* to spread slander and falsehood. One is the way of the people of truth, while the other is the way of the people of innovation. Now, if we speak about the state of Iran, what would people say? Would they say, "This is wrong. Why are you criticizing Iran? Why don't you leave this government alone?" Indeed, they do not criticize Iran now or mention its faults. If they mention them, they simply say, "It's just the *Shiah*," as if they are indifferent. Do they even highlight the faults of the *Shiah* now?

They (those who avoid criticizing Iran) never mention how the *Shiah* treat the weak and needy of *Ahl al-Sunnah* who live among them. Do they speak about what happens in their schools? Do they mention what they have done to the schools of *Ahl al-Sunnah*? They say nothing about any of this. All they do is direct their anger at this country (i.e., Saudi Arabia), purely for the sake of creating discord—not out of sincerity to Allah, His Book, or the *Ummah*. Rather, it is to incite unrest and stir *fitnah* in this land, just as agitators do in every time and place.

As for us, we offer sincere advice. Once, someone came to me and said, 'O *Shaykh*, I went to such-and-such a place and found a well around which the pilgrims gathered, drawing water from it, washing themselves, sprinkling their clothes, and doing this and that. They call it 'She-Camel's Well.' We said, 'Write about it.' Praise be to Allah. All our students take part in groups to enjoin good, forbid evil, and inform the authorities about wrongdoing. They are busy with this. All praise is for Allah.

Through Allah's favor, we have leaders among us to whom we can clarify matters, write, and offer advice. If they fulfill their duty, then all praise is due to Allah. If not, we have still done our part. By Allah's grace, we do not remain silent about wrongdoing. We collaborate to eliminate evils they may not even realize as wrongs. However, some seek to stir up discord rather than truly enjoin good and forbid evil.

Throughout history, figures such as Ibn Saba', Ibn Tumart, Abu Muslim al-Khurasani, 'Ali b. al-Fadl, and even Mustafa Kemal Atatürk have outwardly portrayed themselves as supporters of Islam. Many political activists in this era and earlier have pretended to uphold Islam, displaying zeal for enjoining good and forbidding evil, but once they achieved their goals, their true intentions became apparent.

As the poet said,

He prayed and fasted for what he wanted,
But when it came, he stopped praying and fasting.

This is a well-known principle: If you see people displaying excessive zeal that deviates from the methodology of the *Salaf,* know that they are united upon desires and innovation.

By Allah, are they more protective of the religion of Allah than the scholars of Islam today? No, by Allah, they are not. What we mentioned about Sudan and Afghanistan proves their lack of sincerity. This exposes the realities and reveals the hidden intentions behind these contradictions and the double standards. This unveils the truth for you.

In the past, the people of desires only had their contradictions exposed after they ascended to power. However, these individuals have been exposed by Allah, Who revealed their contradictions and desires even before they achieved their goals. We ask Allah to place a barrier between them and what they seek.

These people are opponents of the *Salafi* methodology and its adherents. To them, the *Salafi* methodology is ineffective and irrelevant—criticizing graves, innovation, and so on— thousands of statements aimed at distorting the *Salafi* methodology, its scholars, and even this state (i.e., Saudi Arabia) because it supports that methodology. This is the core of the matter if you understand it. By Allah, it is not about opposing wrongdoing. They are liars. If they truly opposed wrongdoing, they would have opposed Sudan and Afghanistan before this state. Does not Afghanistan cultivate *hashish*? Are not hashish and opium, which the Jews and Christians outlaw, grown in Afghanistan? Thousands of graves were built there, and the number of graves multiplied after the conflict. During the conflict, they used the wealth of Muslims to construct these graves. Can you expect such people to establish a state upon *tawhid*?

Do you know of any ruler in this country upon whose grave a shrine has been built? No. Whenever the government is informed of a grave, they say, "Demolish it," following the way of Muhammad (ﷺ). Wrongdoings are opposed, innovations are combated, and the symbols of Islam are upheld. Shops close fifteen to thirty minutes before prayer in some places. Does this exist anywhere else in the world? Go to any other country, and you will find people eating, drinking, consuming alcohol, committing adultery, and dancing during the day in Ramadan. Do you see anything like that here?

The people of innovation carry out their practices in basements and hidden places, unable to declare their innovations openly—be they from the *Rafidah*, the *Sufis*, or others. Do you find anything like this in other countries? Here, the books of the people of innovation are banned. Praise be to Allah. We ask Allah to purify this land from the deceptive books of the Muslim Brotherhood. To this day, the scholars of this country have not fully realized that the books of the Muslim Brotherhood are more dangerous than those of all other innovators. This is because they have not read them. They would act if they knew and understood this. May Allah guide them to remove these books and protect our youth from them. Currently, there is nothing more dangerous to the youth of this *Ummah* than the ideas and innovations of the Muslim Brotherhood.

We are in a good state, though evil has existed in all Islamic eras. Even during the Umayyad period, many people were ignorant of the prohibition of alcohol, as *Shaykh Al-Islam* Ibn Taymiyyah mentioned. Yet here, praise be to Allah, the lawful and unlawful are evident because of the guidance of scholars and schools built upon the true methodology of "Allah said," and "His Messenger said." This clarity enrages the people of innovation, including the Muslim Brotherhood, who yearn for a day when "Allah said" and "His Messenger said" no longer prevail. These proofs demolish their innovations and those of their allies among the misguided. They resent hearing statements like "Ibn Taymiyyah said," "Ibn 'Abd Al-Wahhab said," or "Ahmad b. Hanbal said," and they dream of the day when such teachings are silenced, leaving only the words of Sayyid Qutb, Al-Mawdudi, Zaynab al-Ghazali, Khomeini, and their likes.

May Allah's blessings and peace be upon our Prophet Muhammad (ﷺ), his family, and his companions.

All praise is for Allah, Lord of all the worlds.

Made in the USA
Middletown, DE
21 January 2025

69099871R00050